TRACK TRUCKS!

JOANNE MATTERN

HIGH
interest
books

Children's Press
A Division of Scholastic Inc.
New York / Toronto / London / Auckland / Sydney
Mexico City / New Delhi / Hong Kong
Danbury, Connecticut

Book Design: Michelle Innes
Contributing Editor: Geeta Sobha
Photo Credits: Cover © Jonathan Ferrey/Getty Images, p. 4 © Streeter Lecka/Getty Images; pp. 6-7 © Chris Stanford/Getty Images; p. 10 © A.Y. Owen/Time Life Pictures/Getty Images; pp. 12-13, 25 © Rusty Jarrett/Getty Images; p. 14 © Jamie Squire/Getty Images; p. 17 © Ronald Martinez/Getty Images; p. 20 © J. Pat Carter/AP/Wide World Photos; pp. 21, 23 © Robert Laberge/Getty Images; p. 22 © Mike McCarn/AP/Wide World Photos; p. 29 © Darrell Ingham/Getty Images; p. 30 © Chris Stanford/Getty Images; p. 32 © Orlin Wagner/AP/Wide World Photos; p. 35 © Tengku Bahar/AFP/Getty Images; p. 38 © Jamie Squire/Getty Images; p. 39 © Scott Olson/Getty Images.

Library of Congress Cataloging-in-Publication Data

Mattern, Joanne, 1963—
    Track trucks! / Joanne Mattern.
    p. cm. - (Stock car racing)
    Includes index.
    ISBN-10: 0-531-16809-3 (lib. bdg.)   0-531-18717-9 (pbk.)
    ISBN-13: 978-0-531-16809-7 (lib. bdg.)   978-0-531-18717-3 (pbk.)
    1. Truck racing-Juvenile literature. 2. Stock cars (Automobiles)-Juvenile literature. I. Title. II. Series.

GV1034.996.M38 2007
796.7-dc22

                                                            2006004997

2 3 4 5 6 7 8 9 10 R 11 10 09 08 07

TABLE OF CONTENTS

The start of a NASCAR Craftsman Truck Series race is one of sport's most exciting moments.

Y ou are at the wheel of a truck. Your hands grip the steering wheel. Your foot presses down on the gas pedal. You zoom forward at 150 miles (241 kilometers) per hour. The roar of big truck engines fills your ears. All around you, other trucks are zooming past each other. Trucks crowd ahead of you, but you spot an opening. Your eyes fix on that gap. You give your engine an extra push and break into the lead. You're almost at the finish line. Will your truck be the first to cross the finish line when the checkered flag comes down?

Obviously, you are not driving an ordinary truck on a normal road. You are racing a specially designed truck as part of the NASCAR Craftsman Truck Series. The Craftsman Truck Series races are designed just for pickup trucks. Just like a car race, the Craftsman Truck Series is all about speed and skill.

NASCAR stands for the National Association for Stock Car Auto Racing. Stock cars and trucks are similar to the cars and trucks people drive every day. The cars and trucks are even made by the same companies that make passenger vehicles. The difference is that NASCAR cars and trucks are built for speed!

The Craftsman Truck Series is a special part of the NASCAR family. It is also the organization's newest member. Let's find out more about NASCAR's newest races and what it is like to be a Craftsman Truck driver!

These joyous crew members celebrated the 2006 Daytona International Speedway victory of their driver, Mark Martin, by climbing the fence!

CHAPTER ONE

RACING AROUND

Car races have been around since the late 1800s. Most of the vehicles used were built just for racing. During the 1930s, however, people began racing the same cars and trucks they used every day. These cars were known as stock cars because they came directly from the dealer's stock.

During the 1930s and 1940s, there were many stock

car races in the United States. These races were especially popular in the southeastern part of the country. However, there were no real rules for stock car races. Races could be held on any track—no matter its condition. There was no official schedule. There were also no rules regarding what kind of vehicles could be raced.

Bill France, Sr., a stock car race promoter, wanted to create one standard racing series. In 1948, France and a man named Ed Otto founded NASCAR. They held the first NASCAR race at the Charlotte Speedway in North Carolina on June 19, 1949.

FIRST TRACK TRUCKS

NASCAR became very popular over time. For almost fifty years, NASCAR featured car racing only. Things changed in 1993. A group of drivers wanted to design pickup trucks especially for racing. They built some NASCAR-style pickup trucks. These trucks were based on stock models. Some of these trucks were put on display during the 1994 Daytona 500. Actual truck races were held later that year. These races showed off how well the new trucks performed.

NASCAR officials knew that truck manufacturers would be excited to be a part of a truck racing series. These companies would want to build trucks for these races. They would sponsor racing teams, too.

NASCAR also knew that fans would find truck racing fun and exciting. In 1995, NASCAR created a series of races just for pickup trucks. They called these races the Super Truck Series. In 1996, the name was changed to the Craftsman Truck Series.

Since its beginnings in 1995, NASCAR truck racing has given fans plenty of excitement and thrills!

At the time the Truck Series was created, most NASCAR races were held in the southeastern states. NASCAR wanted to branch out to other parts of the country. These races would be a way to introduce new audiences to the sport. NASCAR chose Phoenix, Arizona, as the site for its first truck race. That race was held on February 5, 1995, at the Phoenix International Raceway.

PICKING UP SPEED

Most races during the first year of the Truck Series were held on short tracks. These tracks were less than 1 mile (1.6 km) long. Until 2001, a few races were even held on road courses. Road course races take place in the streets. Many of these early races were less than 125 miles (241 km) long. Drivers would do 150 laps on short tracks.

In 1998, trucks started racing on speedways. These tracks are at least 1 mile (1.6 km) long. Most of these races were held at tracks that also hosted Winston Cup and Busch Series car races.

Today, Craftsman Truck Series races are longer than they were in the 1990s. Most Craftsman Truck Series races are about 250 miles (402 km) long at larger tracks. At medium-sized tracks, the races can be

150 to 200 miles (241 to 322 km) long. The shortest tracks feature races that last 200 to 250 laps.

THE RULES OF TRUCK RACING

When the truck series started in 1995, officials made some new rules. These rules were not the same as rules in stock car racing. Unlike other NASCAR races, there

Truck series pit crews are highly skilled people who work hard and fast!

were no pit stops in the truck series at first. The pits are where the pit crew work on the racing car or truck during a race. The crew changes the vehicle's tires. They also refuel the vehicle and make minor repairs.

NASCAR officials were concerned about safety. Some of the tracks where truck racing took place did not have pit areas that were safe enough for stops.

Some did not have pit areas on the tracks at all. Instead, truck teams took a 10-minute halftime break to make any changes. Of course, emergency stops, such as tire changes, were allowed.

NASCAR tried out many plans for pit stops and breaks. The single halftime break was changed to two breaks during short races in 1996. Longer races got

This NASCAR official waves the green flag, marking either the beginning of a race or the resumption of the race after a break in the action.

three breaks. Trucks were allowed to stop twice for refueling at certain points, and a third stop was given at the halfway point of the race. At this time, crews could refuel and change tires. These limits on tire changes had a big effect on the race. Drivers had to learn how to drive to save their tires so they would last for half the race.

In 1997, NASCAR started allowing pit stops through-out truck races. The trucks were only allowed to refuel during these stops. Tire changes had to be made during a break or an emergency. The next year, NASCAR introduced caution periods—times when a race is run under a yellow warning flag. Teams could change up to four tires during these caution periods.

OVERTIME

The Craftsman Truck Series also had special rules for ending races. In 2004, NASCAR introduced a new overtime rule. Drivers have one try to end the race in a "green-white-checkered" finish. A green-white-checkered finish applies to the last two laps of a race after the race has been stopped. The first of these two laps is started by a green flag. Then the final lap is run under a white flag—the signal for the last lap of a race. If an incident calling for a yellow flag occurs during these laps, the race ends right away.

These special rules set the Craftsman Truck Series apart from other NASCAR races. They made the races very exciting. Drivers had to use a lot of strategy to do well in a race. Fans loved the surprises and the action. The series attracted new fans to NASCAR. Soon the Craftsman Truck Series was a NASCAR star in its own right.

FAST FACT

Mike Skinner won the first truck race in Phoenix. He went on to win that year's truck series championship. Later, Skinner competed in NASCAR's top car race series.

NASCAR FLAGS

The flags used during NASCAR races have special meanings.

Green flag: The start of a race

Yellow flag: Racing conditions are hazardous

Red flag: The race must stop and the pit crews must stop their work

Black flag: (also called the consultation flag): Drivers must stop for a rule violation

Black flag with white X: Drivers who do not stop after being shown the black are in serious rule violation

Blue with orange Stripe: A slower driver must let faster drivers pass

White flag: The last lap of the race

Checkered flag: The end of the race

CHAPTER TWO

A DIFFERENT KIND OF TRUCK

Craftsman Truck Series vehicles are based on stock models of ordinary pickup trucks. However, there is nothing ordinary about a Craftsman truck! A racing truck is very different from the pickup truck in your neighbor's driveway. Everything about a Craftsman Truck is geared for speed—and winning.

BIGGER AND FASTER

The most important difference between a NASCAR truck and a regular pickup truck is horsepower. Horsepower is the amount of power an engine has. A passenger truck's horsepower is about 160. A racing truck's horsepower is an amazing 710! That means a racing truck can go a lot faster than a passenger truck.

Racing trucks are longer and wider than passenger trucks. An average passenger truck is about 194.5 inches (494 centimeters) long and 77 inches (196 cm) wide. A NASCAR truck is 222 inches (564 cm) long and about 80 inches (203 cm) wide.

NASCAR trucks are a lot shorter than passenger trucks. A NASCAR truck is only about 59 inches (150 cm) high. A passenger truck is about 70 inches (178 cm) high. NASCAR trucks are built to be much closer to the ground than passenger trucks. Racing trucks also weigh less than passenger trucks. A passenger truck weighs almost 4,000 pounds (1,814 kg)! They are built to pull heavy-duty loads. A racing truck only weighs 3,400 pounds (1542 kg). This lighter, low-riding truck creates less drag and moves a lot faster than a passenger truck.

A NEED FOR SPEED

The many parts of NASCAR trucks are built especially for racing. Racing trucks have bigger engines than passenger trucks. All engines have cylinders. The more cylinders an engine has, the more power it provides. A passenger truck engine usually has six cylinders. A NASCAR truck's engine has eight cylinders. That bigger engine gives the NASCAR truck more power and speed.

Skilled mechanics such as this one work on the huge, high-powered truck engines.

A NASCAR truck's bed is covered. A covered bed has less resistance to wind, helping the truck go faster. This is important when the driver has to reach speeds of 190 miles (306 km) per hour.

To keep the truck steady at such high speeds, NASCAR trucks have a metal blade called a spoiler on the back. This spoiler can be moved to change the air flowing over the vehicle. It also keeps the truck from skidding back and forth on the track.

Driver David Starr climbs from his truck at a speedway in Concord, North Carolina. Notice the metal blade, or spoiler, on the back of David's vehicle.

NASCAR'S RACING SPONSOR

NASCAR's other racing series are the Nextel Cup Series and the Busch Series. Each racing series has its own sponsor. The Nextel Cup Series is sponsored by Nextel, a telecommunications company. The Busch Series' sponsor is Anheuser-Busch, a beer-brewing company. Craftsman, the truck racing sponsor, is a company that makes household tools.

SAFETY FEATURES

A NASCAR truck has some interesting safety features. Like NASCAR race cars, racing trucks have doors that do not open. The drivers enter through the windows. The windshield on racing trucks is made of special shatterproof glass. Nylon netting covers the side windows instead of breakable glass. There are support bars on the back of the truck. These are part of a steel tube

Driver Ted Musgrave settles in behind the wheel, wearing his helmet and special harness that acts as the driver's seat belt.

roll cage. This cage protects the driver if the truck rolls over. An additional metal safety cage inside the car gives extra protection.

All drivers must wear a seat belt. Racing drivers need to wear these, too. The difference is that they wear a heavy harness instead of a simple seat belt. Two straps of the harness go over the driver's shoulders. Two more go around the waist and one goes between the legs. All NASCAR drivers must use the HANS device. HANS stands for Head and Neck Support. This prevents neck injuries.

FAST FACT

NASCAR trucks do not have headlights. Instead, special stickers called decals are used in place of lights.

CHAPTER THREE

CRAFTSMAN DRIVERS

Truck racing was popular from the beginning. Fans soon discovered that this was a rough and exciting style of racing. Craftsman Truck races feature a lot of side-by-side racing. Two or three trucks can race next to each other. When racing at top speed so close to each other, the trucks sometimes bang into each other. These bumps can cause a lot of heart-pounding moments in the races.

When the Craftsman Truck Series started in 1995, most of the drivers had a lot of experience. They had raced stock cars on short tracks. Still, they had not been able to break into other areas of NASCAR racing. Racing trucks gave these drivers a chance to develop their skills on longer tracks.

OPPORTUNITY TO RACE

These drivers got a lot of experience racing NASCAR pickup trucks. Many of them went on to race in other NASCAR series. Most of the drivers who won Craftsman Truck championships during the 1990s went on to race in the Nextel Cup. The Nextel Cup is one of NASCAR's most famous stock car racing series. Greg Biffle, Scott Riggs, Kevin Harvick, Kurt Busch, Kyle Busch, and Carl Edwards are just a few famous NASCAR drivers who got their start in the Craftsman Truck Series.

Some drivers who were retired from NASCAR's Nextel/Winston Cup Series decided to join the Craftsman Truck Series, too. These drivers were no longer racing cars, and they found that they could make a good living racing trucks. Older racers also enjoyed the Craftsman Truck Series' shorter schedule.

They could keep racing, but they had more time to spend with their families, too. Racing in the Craftsman Truck Series helps these drivers find the best of both worlds.

MEET SOME CRAFTSMAN TRUCK SERIES DRIVERS!

Bobby Hamilton was a top Winston Cup racer for twelve seasons. In 1997, Hamilton bought his own Craftsman Truck and started a team. The team was called Bobby Hamilton Racing. Hamilton went on to own three truck teams. In 2003, Hamilton decided to get behind the wheel himself. He started racing his own trucks and won many races. In 2004, Hamilton became the oldest champion in Craftsman Truck history. He was forty-seven years old.

Ted Musgrave is another veteran driver. During the 1990s, Musgrave was a top Winston Cup driver. In 2001, Musgrave joined Jim Smith's team. He got behind the wheel of one of Smith's Dodge Ram pickup trucks. He won seven Craftsman races in 2001. By the end of that first year, he was in second place for the season championship. In 2005, Musgrave won the championship. He said that truck racing had given him "the chance to go out and win some races and have fun."

Ted Musgrave celebrates his 2005 championship win at the NASCAR Truck Series Ford 200 in Homestead, Florida.

Jack Sprague is the only driver to win three season championships in Craftsman Truck racing. He won in 1997, 1999, and 2001. In 2001, he beat Ted Musgrave

Bill Lester has raced trucks and cars. Here he is at the Atlanta Motor Speedway in 2006 before the start of a race.

for the championship. No one has won more prize money in the Craftsman Truck Series.

Bill Lester became NASCAR's only full-time African American driver in 2003. Lester started out in road races. In 2002, Bobby Hamilton asked Lester to drive one of his Dodge trucks. Lester did very well. He hopes his presence will bring other African Americans into NASCAR racing, too.

FAST FACT

Kyle Busch was thrown out of a 2001 Craftsman Truck Series race in California. Why? Officials discovered he was only sixteen years old. A rule said drivers had to be eighteen years old.

Kelly Sutton set the record as the woman with the highest number of races under her belt in 2005. Sutton won the Most Popular Driver Award in 2002. That same year, she was the third runner-up for rookie of the year and was number twelve in the points standings. Kelly is also the first person with

Kelly Sutton poses for the cameras before a meeting with members of the press at the Daytona International Speedway in 2006.

multiple sclerosis, a nerve disorder that is rare in women, known to race in any NASCAR series.

FAMILY AFFAIR

Some Craftsman Truck drivers come from racing families. Jon Wood is one of these drivers. His family is one of the most important families in NASCAR. His grandfather was Glen Wood, the cofounder of Wood Brothers Racing. Jon Wood grew up around race cars. His first races, however, were not in cars or trucks. They were in go-carts! Wood started racing go-carts when he was twelve years old. Soon he was the national champion. Wood began racing in the Craftsman Series when he was twenty years old in 2001. He became one of the hottest rookies in the sport.

RACING TEAM

Behind each driver of the NASCAR racing teams is a crew of people, each performing their own important job:

Team Owner: Pays for the racing vehicle and handles the money, bills, and payroll

Team Manager: Hires and manages team members

Crew Chief: Responsible for directing the pit crew

Engine Specialist: Maintains the vehicle's engine

Pit Crew Members: Gas person, catch-can person (responsible for catching spilled fuel while gas is being filled), tire carrier, tire changer, and jackman (responsible for the hydraulic jack that lifts the car for tire changes).

COMING UP THE TRACK

There are many young drivers who can't wait to get into the NASCAR action! NASCAR has a junior division for these drivers. Some of them race in the FASCAR Pro Sport Pickup Truck Division. FASCAR stands for Florida Association of Stock Car Racing. Here drivers as young as twelve years old can learn to drive racing trucks. They work with older drivers. Meanwhile, NASCAR is watching them. The young drivers of today are tomorrow's stars!

It takes a team of dedicated and skilled racing professionals to win the big races!

CHAPTER FOUR

TRUCKS AND OWNERS

NASCAR truck racing could not exist without the truck manufacturers and sponsors that are involved. The truck manufacturers know how to design and build these amazing trucks to win races. The sponsors and the owners provide the money that racing teams need. Running a team can cost as much as twenty million dollars a year! Some racing trucks and cars may have more than one sponsor.

THE COMPANY YOU KEEP

Ford, Chevrolet, Dodge, and Toyota are the companies that make trucks that compete in the Craftsman Truck Series. These companies also race stock cars in NASCAR's other divisions. The Dodge Ram is probably the best-known truck in NASCAR. It has won more Craftsman Truck Series races than any other type of truck.

NASCAR race cars must be manufactured in the United States. In 2004, Toyota was the first foreign manufacturer to join the Truck Series. The company is based in Japan, but the Toyota Tundra truck is built in the United States. Toyota also made the Craftsman Truck Series the only NASCAR series with four manufacturers. The company won its first Craftsman race in August 2004. At that race, there were three Toyota Tundras in the top five.

PUTTING UP THE CASH

Another important part of NASCAR racing is the owner. Owners lead the racing teams. They own the trucks that the drivers race. In 2005, there were more than twenty-five different racing teams and owners in the Craftsman Truck Series. Owners put a lot of money into their cars and teams.

Many of these owners are former race car drivers. Bobby Hamilton, Darrell Waltrip, and Jack Roush are just a few of the drivers who now own truck teams. Other owners are family members of famous drivers. These owners include Stephanie Hamilton and DeLana Harvick. One person may own several different trucks.

Sometimes celebrities become owners, too. In 2003, hip-hop star Nelly announced that he would buy into a Craftsman Truck Series team. Nelly bought part of Billy Ballew Motorsports. Nelly had been a racing fan for many years. He was excited about becoming part of the sport. Nelly also hoped that he could bring more African Americans to the exciting world of truck racing.

FAST FACT

The 1995 Craftsman Truck Series champion Mike Skinner earned $428,096. In 2005, champion Ted Musgrave won $880,553.

Hip-hop star Nelly is a big fan of NASCAR racing.

Owners, drivers, trucks, officials, and fans are all important parts of NASCAR's Craftsman Truck Series. Next time you see a pickup truck, think about how fast a NASCAR truck can go. Then let your imagination fly down the track!

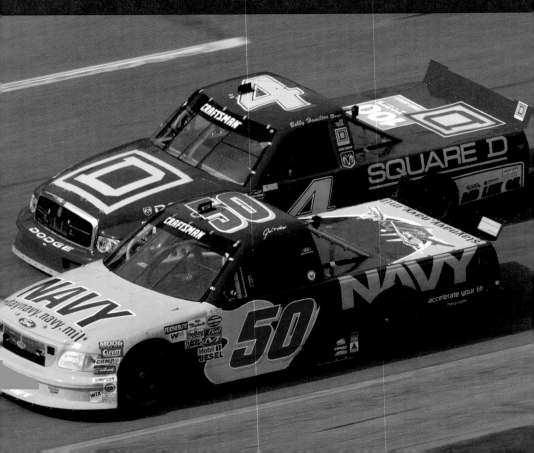

Bobby Hamilton (in the #4 truck) is one of many former stock car drivers who have become owners—and drivers—of truck teams.

CHART

Craftsman Truck Series vehicles are different from
regular trucks. However, in many ways, they are a
lot like Nextel Cup cars. Here's how a Ford F150
pickup and a Nextel Cup car match up:

SPECS	CRAFTSMAN TRUCK	NEXTEL CUP CAR
Wheelbase	112 inches (2.8 m)	110 inches (2.7 m)
Horsepower	770	770
Top speed	190 mph (306 kph)	200 mph (322 kph)
Weight	3400 pounds (1,542 kg)	3400 pounds
Length	194 inches (495 cm)	200 inches (511 cm)
Width	75 inches (19 cm)	72.5 inches (184 cm)
Height	59 inches (150 cm)	51 inches (130 cm)
Rear Spoiler	67.76 inches wide (173 cm) 8 inches tall (20 cm)	55 inches wide (140 cm) 6.25 inches tall (16 cm)

NEW WORDS

cylinder (**sil**-uhn-dur) a chamber in an engine that is shaped like a tube

drag (**drag**) a force that makes an object in motion move more slowly

horsepower (**horss**-pou-ur) the amount of power created by an engine

hydraulic (hye-**draw**-lik) power that is created by liquid being forced under pressure

incident (**in**-suh-dugnt) something that happens

lap (**lap**) one time around a racetrack

passenger trucks (**pass**-uhn-jur **truhks**) trucks used for everyday purposes and driven on roads

pit (**pit**) the place on the side of a racetrack where cars and trucks are refueled and repaired

pit crew (**pit kroo**) members of a car racing team who make repairs and refuel the race car

refuel (ree-**fyoo**-uhl) to refill a car with gasoline

NEW WORDS

resistance (ri-ziss-tuhnss) a force, such as wind, that opposes the motion of an object

road races (rohd rays-uhs) races held on roads rather than racetracks

roll cage (rohl kayj) steel tubes inside a race car that protect the driver if the car rolls over

rookie (ruk-ee) someone who is new at a sport

runner-up (ruhn-ur up) the person or team that comes in second in a race or competition

short track (short trak) a racetrack that is less than 1 mile (1.6 km) long

speedway (speed-way) a race track that is at least 1 mile (1.6 km) long

spoiler (spoil-uhr) a metal blade attached to the back of a car or truck to change the way air flows over the vehicle

veteran (vet-ur-uhn) someone who has been doing something for a long time

FOR FURTHER READING

Buckley, James, Jr. *Eyewitness NASCAR*. New York: DK
   Publishing, Inc., 2005.

Fresina, Michael. *For the Love of NASCAR: An A-to-Z Primer
   for NASCAR Fans of All Ages*. Chicago, IL: Triumph
   Books, 2005.

Woods, Bob. *NASCAR: The Greatest Races*. Pleasantville, NY:
   Reader's Digest Children's Publishing, Inc., 2004.

Woods, Bob. *Pit Pass: Behind the Scenes of NASCAR*.
   Pleasantville, NY: Reader's Digest, 2005.

The Official NASCAR Handbook. New York: HarperCollins
   Publishers, 1998.

RESOURCES

ORGANIZATION

NASCAR Craftsman Truck Series
PO Box 2875
Daytona Beach, FL 32120

RESOURCES

WEB SITES

NASCAR

www.nascar.com

This site provides information, photographs, and all the latest NASCAR news.

Truck Series

www.truckseries.com

Learn more about your favorite Truck Series drivers, find out more about the series, and much more at this site.

Jayski's Silly Season Site: Race Tracks

www.jayski.com/links/tracklinks.htm

Read up on all the tracks where NASCAR races are held throughout the United States.

INDEX

INDEX

ABOUT THE AUTHOR

Joanne Mattern has written more than 200 books for children. Her favorite topics include sports, history, animals, and biographies. Joanne lives in New York State with her husband, three daughters, and three cats.